How Women Run Circles around Men

By Blaine Williams

I0413778

Table of Contents

Introduction

Women are pretty good at manipulating men. If you have been manipulated by a woman before, you are far from alone. Women know just how to talk to men to get what they want. Usually, they are successful. You may find yourself the victim of manipulation in relationships as well as your day-to-day interactions with other women. But you don't have to just stand there and let women run circles around you.

You are a human being with basic human rights. You do not owe anyone anything. Therefore, you do not deserve to be manipulated and used like a pawn. Stand up for yourself. Stop letting women hurt you and use you.

Find out how you can protect yourself and preserve your pride with this handy guide. In this book, you will learn to understand women and their manipulative methods better. You will also learn how to stand up to these women and say no. You will no longer be outsmarted by women, either. Your life will be much easier when you are fully in control.

It is part of human nature for men to want to help women. But women are strong, capable creatures. They usually are not weak; if they portray themselves as weak, they are lying and trying to manipulate you. Stop falling for this game. Stop letting your desire to meet women and help women interfere with your judgment.

Instead, take control of your life and be resolute in your will.

Chapter I: How Women Manipulate Men

Women manipulate men in a variety of different ways. They often use their feminine traits to get desired reactions out of men. Often, they put on such a charming, cute, or seductive show that men can't say no to them. Therefore, women have a lot of hidden power over men.

First, let's consider why women like to manipulate men. This background can give you some insight into the motives that women have. Then, you can better understand how to combat this manipulation.

Why Women are Manipulative

After centuries of subjugation in most cultures, a majority of women from around the world have grown accustomed to not having power of any kind. They could not do what they wanted without the permission of a father or husband figure, and they could not tell men what to do. However, women have needs, just like any person. Therefore, women needed a way to get what they wanted. They learned that since direct dominance did not work on men, more subtle persuasion and manipulation was far more effective. Women perfected the art of getting what they wanted without men even vaguely suspecting what was going on.

Fortunately, now, women have really made great strides in the direction of equal rights. Most women are able to get what they want through asking directly and maturely. But the unfortunate side of this coin is that most women have been raised to be cunning and manipulative, without even realizing it. They still feel that they need to manipulate men because they have not been exposed to healthier models of communication. Female generations have passed down the art of subtle manipulation of the male gender, and no better ways of treating men and getting their way have been learned and passed on. It is practically woven into women's communication styles and gender dynamics to be sneaky, manipulative, and indirect.

A lot of women do not even mean to be this way. They do not intend to cause men any harm or frustration. They have simply learned indirect, unclear communication tactics which men find infuriating or puzzling. They have learned to get their way and make suggestions through hints, rather than speaking directly like adults are supposed to. Other women are very aware of how much power they wield with manipulation, and they thoroughly delight in being manipulative. They do not realize that they could have an easier experience and earn more respect if they communicated more directly with men.

In addition, many women use manipulation as a form of power play. They know that they can beat men at mind games and verbal manipulation, so they use that to their advantage to win the imaginary gender war that has existed since the beginning of history. You will find that women enjoy gaining power over you and proving their strength through subtle tactics that you do not possess.

This manipulation that women run is not just caused by gender constructs, however. It is also an evolutionary component of the female sex that stems from Nature, not nurture. Women are biologically programmed to use more emotion in their communication. They like to talk just to talk and they use talking as a way to bond with others. Meanwhile, men approach communication a little differently. Most men use communication to convey facts or solve problems. Feelings and bonding can enter men's communication, but not as much as it does with women. This communication difference alone can lead to epic misunderstandings between the sexes and the perception that women are manipulative.

While women certainly can be manipulative at times, a lot of men think that women are just being that way when women cry or otherwise become emotional during arguments. However, a lot of women are just that way because of their biological hardwiring. They are not intentionally being manipulative; they just naturally communicate emotionally. Their emotional displays often disarm and guilt men, which is why women appear to be manipulative using emotions. But usually women are just emotional in their communication to begin with and this is not a deliberate ploy.

Women also tend to be more intuitive and empathetic than men when it comes to communication. This is why women expect men to know what they are talking about. They drop hints and expect men to understand. Women expect men to be mind readers because they possess natural intuition, but men do not have the same capability. Often, men like to be told things exactly. They do not understand hints and they cannot read minds. It can appear that women are being very manipulative when they drop these hints and get mad when men fail to accurately guess what they mean, but in fact they are just expecting men to be more like themselves in communication. The idea that men just cannot think and communicate the same way as women simply does not occur to them.

Don't make the mistake of thinking that women are entirely innocent, however. A lot of women are completely aware of the communication differences between men and them. They exploit these differences in a form of power play. They have found that they can use these communication differences for their own advantage, at the expense of the men that they manipulate. Women will intentionally cause misunderstandings or pretend to not understand what men are saying. They will also pretend to be overly emotional just to get men to do what they want.

Some women are absolute monsters. There is no point sugar coating this fact. You have quite possibly dated someone who was psychotic, deliberately hurtful, and extremely manipulative. You probably never knew what this woman's plan was, but somehow you factored into it and you seemed to only exist for her use. Being used this way is a nasty feeling, but some people are just users. Women who are like this usually suffer from a sociopathic or psychopathic disorder, where they desire and even enjoy harming you and where they feel positively no remorse about manipulating you. Women like this are not normal. They are toxic people that you must avoid at all costs. Do not let a bad experience with a sociopath sour you toward all women, as sociopaths represent only roughly four percent of the total human population.

The manipulations of a sociopathic woman are probably ten times better than that of a normal woman. A sociopath can get you to do anything that she wants. This is why you should avoid such people, as they will use you as tools in their lives and then throw you away when you no longer serve them a useful purpose. A sociopathic woman also will use various games to hurt you, just for her own pleasure and sense of control.

Other mental disorders can make women very manipulative, as well. A co-dependent woman may enjoy being the mothering type, so she does what she can to make you dependent upon her care. She will act like a mother hen, enabling you to do nothing but rely on her. A depressed woman may become very self-absorbed after years spent suffering in quiet misery, so she may manipulate you to serve her and make her feel better. She may also become dependent on you, and will manipulate you just to keep you around. A narcissistic woman secretly fears abandonment and seeks the praise of others, and she will manipulate you to think the world of her.

Women are naturally very nurturing, loving, and caring. It may not seem like it, but most women desire only the best for those around them. For this reason, female family members and friends may become overly invested and over-involved in your life. This is just because they care about you and want the best for you. But their caring manifests in many negative ways, including manipulation. They tend to manipulate you to get you to do what they feel is in your best interests. Whether or not you agree varies on the situation, but you are probably resentful of their manipulation either way. As a grown man, you want to take control of your own life and you do not want to be controlled through subtle mind games by the women in your life. Just understand that women usually have your best interests at heart and are not trying to be mean when they manipulate you. Really, they can't help it because they are genetically programmed to be overprotective, mothering types.

Think of this example: You want to go out at night with your friends but your mother is worried about you getting into legal trouble, getting mugged and shot, or even drinking and driving, so she manipulates you by crying about how you never spend time with her. You assume that she is doing this because she wants to monopolize your time and is jealous of your friends, but in reality she just wants to protect you. She runs manipulation on you to get you to stay home with her instead of going out with your friends because she knows that if she asks you to stay in for your safety, you will just say that you will be fine and then leave anyway.

Finally, some manipulation is really just basic human nature. Men are just as capable of being manipulative as women. Manipulation is a very effective way to get what you want, and many people have figured that out. Many people hide ulterior motives from you and string you along until you help them fulfill their secret plans. You are not aware of the plan that you are so instrumental in. Other times, you may say no, so a woman goes to work persuading you to change your mind and say yes. Being manipulated is never a good feeling. Sadly, you will catch a lot of people trying to manipulate you in life and it will always sting to know that you are little more than a tool to certain people. Manipulation is something both men and women engage in. Even your kids might try to manipulate you to get what they want, such as an extra cookie after dinner. Fortunately, you can learn to spot and deflect this type of manipulation in order to protect your own interests and maintain your self-respect and autonomy. No one, man or woman, will be able to penetrate your shield and use you for his or her own ends after you learn how to protect yourself.

Seduction itself calls for some manipulation. Think about it. You probably use some form of subtle manipulation to seduce women yourself. You do not want to portray the character flaws that you possess or the bad things about yourself to someone that you want to make fall for you. Women are the same way. This is just basic human nature. A woman will show you what she knows that you want to see in order to seduce you and spark your romantic or sexual interest. She will put on a façade designed to charm you. While this is manipulation, it is up to you to decide if you will tolerate it or not. You probably wouldn't want to date anyone if they didn't put on an attractive façade. You have to fall in love with a person very deeply before you are willing to tolerate their flaws and gross habits. Therefore, it is probably acceptable to let women continue to try to manipulate how you see them just for seduction purposes. Just bear in mind that no woman is perfect and that women typically erect carefully assembled facades when you first meet them. Once you get to know a woman, you will almost always discover that the initial impression that you formed of her is not entirely accurate.

These are the main reasons that women run circles around men. From trying to get power over men to simply not realizing what they are doing to having mental disorders, there are many reasons why women can be manipulative. Also remember that women are not the only ones who can be this way; men are perfectly capable of manipulating you and running circles around you as well. However, since the scope of this book is limited to dealing with manipulative women, I will not discuss how or why men can be manipulative or how to protect yourself in that way. Just know that many of the techniques that I cover in this book can be used with men as well as women.

Now I will go into how women can con men. There are so many ways that women can manipulate you that I cannot possibly cover every single manipulation method in this book. However, I will cover the most important and most common forms of manipulation that you are likely to run into. It is crucial for you to know these manipulation techniques so that you can identify them and avoid responding to them. Never give a manipulative woman what she wants if you want to reserve power for yourself. Always resist and/or deflect each of the following manipulation tactics that I am going to cover. I will show you how in a later chapter.

Different Methods Women Use to Manipulate Men

High Pitched Voices

Men naturally respond to the high pitch of female voices. Women have been found to naturally, even subconsciously, increase the pitch of their voices when speaking to men. They do this because somewhere inside, they understand that men will respond to this.

If a woman walks up to you and starts talking to you in a high-pitched voice, watch out. Resist the urge to respond to her just because of how she is speaking to you. Is this her normal voice? Or did she just whip this higher pitched voice out around you to get you to do something for her? Observe women for a while, and you will notice how they raise the pitch of their voices only when they are trying to seduce you or get you to do something.

One thing you should watch for is when a woman suddenly changes her pitch around you for no discernible reason. Why the sudden change? It could be that she wants to jump your bones, which can be great if you want to have sex with her. But it could also be that she is trying to somehow manipulate you or otherwise use you for some end. Is she asking you for something? Did her ex just walk into the room, and now she is trying to act flirty toward you just to make him jealous? Is she on the phone, possibly around a boyfriend or friend that she is trying to make jealous? Is your girlfriend or wife present and she is trying to start trouble in your relationship? You will notice that when a woman starts speaking to you in a higher pitch for no apparent reason, there is a hidden reason. She is just raising her voice in order to somehow manipulate or use you. Don't fall for it and certainly don't assume that she really likes you for who you are. You can even confront her and tell her to speak to you normally, which will certainly burst her bubble and make her stop.

Seduction

Women know that men love the female body. It is just programmed into most heterosexual men to love the curves, lines, and voluptuousness of the female body. Thus, women understand that they can use their bodies to manipulate men. They use sexual seduction to get their way.

Have you ever met a woman who flashes her cleavage around or stretches out her long legs in front of you? This woman is probably trying to manipulate you. She knows that she is hot, and she wants you to notice how good she looks. She thinks that by showing you her skin, you will want to go to bed. In order to go to bed, however, she wants you to believe that you must do something for her. A lot of men will indeed jump through hoops just to get sex. It is a biological thing that I think most men cannot help. But you have control over yourself and you do not need to do things for a woman just to get laid. More often than not, you will find that a woman who asks you to do things for her with the promise of a sexual reward actually never delivers on that reward. A woman who really wants to have sex with you will not require you to do her favors beforehand.

Watch out for women who stroke their throats or chests or run their hands up their bare legs while talking to you. They are just trying to draw your eyes toward different parts of their bodies. Also watch out for women who dress in super sexy clothes. These women are trying to be both subservient and seductive to all men around and they do not respect themselves enough to cover up. They are probably weak and manipulative. Beware.

Finally, if a woman flirts with you, consider that she may have an ulterior motive. Back out if she offers you sex on the condition that you do something for her. Also back out if she asks you to do her a favor in an extremely flirtatious, seductive way. She could just ask you straight up, but she chose to do it in a flirtatious way. You do not deserve to be manipulated. You should be offended by her unwarranted and sneaky attempt to manipulate you with seduction, and you should refuse to do what she asks.

Also, watch your significant other. If you two have a fight and suddenly she starts pouting, bending over in front of you, or otherwise showing off her body, she may be trying to get you to forgive her by distracting you with her body. She thinks that sex will make you forget how nasty she is being toward you. Do not let this sexy act distract you. Continue to hash out any serious issues that you must contend with and do not shy away from confronting her over how abysmally she has been treating you. You do not have to chase after sex with her just because she wants it. There is time for that later. Do not fall for this very common manipulation by seduction.

Touching

Another common form of manipulation that you should watch out for is when women start using subtle touch on you. She may touch your arm during a commercial about a diamond collection at Jared's. She may touch you during an argument to get you to simmer down. She may touch you just to forge some sort of connection so that you are more likely to give her what she wants.

Touch establishes familiarity. It can also start the seduction process, though not always. I put touch in a separate section from seduction because it really is separate from seduction. Women may use touch to get you horny, but they may also just use it to establish false warmth and familiarity so that you will feel more inclined to do what they want. You do not have to do anything and you should not assume that there is any warmth or familiarity between you two just because she touches you. It is natural for you to think that, but resist the thought. This is just manipulation, subconscious or conscious.

Women may also use touch just to get your attention. You do not have to fall for this. A woman does not require your constant attention, so you can confront her about grabbing your elbow all of the time just so that you look at her.

Pretending to Need Help

It is natural for you to want to rush to the aid of a helpless damsel in distress. Your protective instincts kick into overdrive when you encounter a woman who needs your help. You may go to great lengths and inconvenience yourself for a woman, just because your instincts override your reason.

Many people claim that men like to help women just to get laid. We both know that this is not true. You may be more inclined to help a woman who is attractive to you or who dangles the opportunity of some sort of physical connection in front of you, but you are probably also inclined to help anyone who really needs it. You like to be nice and you like to feel useful. You want to do your part to help the world.

But whatever your motivation is for assisting others, understand that women especially understand how badly you like to help. They exploit this in order to be lazy. They will use you to avoid doing things themselves. There are many women who view men as paychecks or work horses and leave everything on men's shoulders.

Another thing that you should consider is that you are enabling women to be weak and dependent on the male sex when you readily offer your help to them. Women nowadays are typically more independent and more willing to do things themselves. They are taking on jobs and educations that were completely male-dominated just fifty years ago. This is great for the equal rights movement. The women who fail to do things for themselves are really just failing this movement and even holding it back. They are continuing to subjugate themselves to men by shirking duties and work onto men. They are pretending to be incompetent just to get men to do things for them, which in turn makes women as a whole look bad and holds back the equal rights movement.

Here is a classic example of what I am talking about that I am guilty of myself. I am not typically a lazy or manipulative person. However, I absolutely hate heavy lifting and I hate changing tires. When I have to do a task that calls for lifting or when I have to change a tire, I can and will do it if I have no other choice. But if there is a man around, I will just automatically ask him to do it for me. I pretend to not have the upper body strength or the knowledge of how to change a tire. Really, I do, but I just hate the work. Men are usually more than willing to jump in and help me. Is this wrong of me? Well, I will let you be the judge of that. But just know that most women are strong, smart, and capable. They simply pretend to be otherwise to shirk the labor onto you.

Indeed, a lot of women cannot lift heavy weights. Women really do not have the same anatomy as men, and therefore they do not have as much physical strength. But women are often a lot stronger than they let on. Do not fall for the weak act that women pull. You can help a woman out with some heavy lifting if you want, but understand that you do not have to. She is probably capable of doing it herself. If it inconveniences you, you can go ahead and say no.

Also, do not fall for the dumb blonde act. A lot of women are great at pretending to be stupid in order to get men to help them and think for them. This is just the same as shirking physical tasks onto the shoulders of men. While there are certainly some women out there with limited intelligence or even mental disabilities who genuinely cannot think for themselves, most women can and do think for themselves. The dumb blonde act is usually just a manipulation tactic. Avoid women who act like this, as they probably are actually very cunning and calculating and have a plan to use you. You can test her intelligence by asking her questions about her life, education, and any books that you may have read. If she really does not seem to have a high IQ, then there is a chance that this is not an act, but more often than not, it is an act that most men are more than happy to buy into.

Any woman who constantly brings up her money troubles around you and makes you feel like you should help her out financially is also just manipulating you. Instead of taking responsibility for her own income and her own bills, she wants a man to provide for her. She makes you feel sorry for her so that you pitch in some money to help her out. You will probably never see that money again and you may or may not hear from her again. But if you do see her again, she will probably be even more shameless in asking for an even bigger loan. Women are perfectly able to work and provide for themselves, so don't let a gold digger convince you otherwise with her sob stories. She is probably just lazy and trying to get a sugar daddy.

However, this is not to say that you should never help women. If you want to, go ahead. Sometimes you will like someone enough that helping her out is a pleasure, rather than a nuisance. Sometimes you encounter someone who is in legitimate need of help. There are women out there who really have hit hard times, or who really do not know how to change a tire. But it is entirely up to you whether or not you should help a woman. Do not feel obligated to help anyone. You can change how dependent upon and manipulative women are to men by refusing to accept their manipulations and offering help whenever you are asked.

Nagging

The most common complaint that men have about their wives is the nagging. Women do tend to nag ceaselessly. Really, this is the same tactic that small children use. A scientific study found that parents usually relent to their children's demands after being asked a total of nine times. Women have also figured out that they can eventually get men to relent if they ask enough times.

You do not have to tolerate nagging. Nagging is disrespectful and unpleasant. Ask your wife or girl or any other woman in your life to stop nagging at you. Show her that you mean business by refusing to do things the more that she nags. Let each time that she brings something up harden your resolve not to do it. She will learn quickly that nagging is not helpful if you refuse to do what she asks you to do more than once. However, sometimes men take a while to get things done, and women get frustrated. This is why they ask more than once, because they feel that something is not going to get done. You can greatly reduce her level of nagging by giving her a time frame of when you will get something done and then sticking to that time frame.

Silent Treatment

The silent treatment is a horrible form of manipulation that is very hurtful. I grew up dealing with the silent treatment from my mother, so I know how hurtful it is. You feel like you are walking on eggshells around the person. You feel like you have no control and like you are the worst scum alive on the planet. Women love using the silent treatment as a way to gain control. They cut off all warmth and love so that you crave their attention. Eventually, you will cave and apologize or do whatever they want, just to get the silent treatment to end. You will also probably take great strides to avoid the silent treatment in the future.

It is better to not let the silent treatment go on. If you do what a woman wants to avoid the silent treatment, then you teach her that she can use this method to effectively manipulate you again in the future. Instead of falling for her silent treatment, flip the tables on her. Go out with your friends, don't talk to her, and don't text her. If she doesn't text you for days, that is fine. The whole time she will be waiting to hear from you. Your radio silence will drive her crazy. Eventually she will probably break her own silent treatment to yell at you, and then you at least have some form of communication again. Adults communicate, children pout and stay silent. So don't play her game. Make her become an adult and actually communicate with you about what she wants. Also, teach her that the silent treatment just does not work on you.

Dropping Hints

Women love to drop hints. Then they get upset when men don't understand or respond to their hints. She might glance at you a certain way during a commercial to let you know that she wants the product being advertised for her birthday next week, and then when you don't get her the product, she pouts and cries and throws a tantrum like a little kid.

Why tolerate this? If a woman really wants something, she should tell you. Adults know that mind reading is impossible and that honesty is required for good communication. Teach her a lesson in adult communication by refusing to acknowledge her hints. When she hints about something, don't respond. Then, when she throws a fit, simply tell her that she needs to tell you things clearly from now on or else you cannot be expected to know what she wants. A grown up woman will fall into line, but an immature one will simply tell you that you need to learn to read her body language and get to know her better. Or she may tell that you should just know things. You don't need such immature women in your life. Don't complicate things and give yourself a headache by trying to learn to read her hints. Instead, continue ignoring her hints and telling her to be straight with you until she finally learns her lesson or else move on to a more mature, upfront woman.

Comparing You to Other Men

One nasty way that women try to get men to become who they want is by comparing them to other men. This can be especially awful if you have a mother who compares you to her friends' children, or a wife who compares you to other available men. It makes you feel like you are not good enough. This is the woman's exact intention.

When a woman compares you to other men, feel free to tell her that it is not cool and that you refuse to be compared to others. Say that you are who you are and you are not this other guy that she is talking about. She is just trying to hurt you and threaten you by offering these comparisons; but there is no real threat. Call her bluff by telling her, "If you like so-and-so so much, why don't you go marry him?"

For instance, your wife may compare you to Darren. She talks about what a nice car Darren drives in some twisted attempt to get you to work harder and pull in more money. She believes that by comparing you to Darren, you will feel bad about yourself and you will thus work harder in order to be like Darren. But you are not Darren and you don't have to be more like him. You also deserve a wife who is honest with you, not someone who tries to manipulate you by hurting your feelings and threatening your ego. So respond by reminding her that you are not Darren and that she can go be with Darren if she wants a richer husband, or else she can start making more money herself to buy that car that she covets. You will be surprised how quickly this rebuff can make a woman stop comparing you to others.

Crying

Remember how I said that women are naturally emotional in their communication?

That is true. Therefore, it is not always a sign of manipulation when a woman bursts into tears around you. Hormones may be another cause of a woman's sudden emotional outburst.

However, some women are great at crying on cue. If actors can do it, then so can some regular people. Women have been known to fake cry or cry on cue just to get you to feel bad. You feel so bad that you lower your guard and do what she wants. You try to fix the problem to make her stop crying, and usually the easiest, clearest way to fix the problem is to give her what she wants.

But you do not have to give a woman what she wants just to help her stop crying. She is responsible for her own emotions. A few tears and hurt feelings will not kill her, if she is truly hurt. Do not let her manipulate you into doing things that you don't want to do just by crying. Even if a woman's tears are genuine, obliging her with what she wants will only teach her that she can cry in the future to get her way with you.

I want to offer a word of caution here, however. Sometimes in love you must make sacrifices. If you really love a woman and you want to be with her, you will sometimes have to give in to her. You do not have to do this all of the time; in fact, you should not do it all of the time. But when you have genuinely messed up and hurt your lady, you must show some compassion when she cries because of you. Otherwise, you will test her patience and maybe even drive her away by being proud and stubborn. She will find that you cannot satisfy her emotional needs and that you do not care if you hurt her or deny her what she needs, so she will eventually give up on you and move on. You really can't blame her if you are continually being insensitive. You do not have to give in to women ever, but you may want to for the sanctity of your relationship. Be discerning and own up to your mistakes. If your wife or girlfriend really wants something that is important to her and that does not hurt you to give, then why not give it to her? It is important to keep the woman that you love happy or you will lose her.

However, the woman that you love needs to take care of your emotions. She should not be exploiting you and manipulating you. If you catch her using fake tears to get her way, then you do not have to give into her. You can confront her for using tears to manipulate you. It is not OK for anyone to manipulate you ever. Keep this attitude and stop tolerating manipulation by women. Usually, you will be able to tell if her tears are real or fake. It is best to respond to real tears and ignore or confront fake ones.

Praising

A lot of men feel that women constantly criticize them. And it is certainly true that women can be very critical of their male loved ones and romantic partners. As a result, you could get a huge ego boost and feel very special when a woman who is normally critical of you starts being extremely nice to you and singing your praises.

A good woman will praise you sometimes just to show that she loves you and that she thinks the world of you. A manipulative woman will only praise you when she wants something. Become cautious when a woman starts praising you. Don't let it get to your head. She is likely to follow her praise up with a request or a confession. You will feel tempted to say yes or to forgive her for what she confesses because she has put you in such a good mood with her praise. But praise is not worth you sacrificing your pride, your feelings, and your control. Do not let praise change or even influence how you respond to a woman. Rather, watch out even more when a woman praises you.

Also watch out for women who routinely try to make you feel special. These women are just trying to bolster your ego. A woman who truly finds you to be special will not have to go to great lengths to make you feel so. She will simply show you that you are special by being sweet to you, taking care of you, and being faithful to you. Therefore, anyone who grooms your ego continually is up to something. Don't fall for her tricks or let her make you believe that you are special. She probably has an entire contact list of guys in her phone that she tries to make feel special so that she can get what she wants.

How Women Outsmart Men

A lot of women get their kicks from being able to outsmart men. When I say outsmart, I mean that women pull one over on you or make you do something without your conscious consent. They are able to fool you and deceive you. It does not necessarily take intelligence to outsmart someone. It simply takes the ability to use the resources at hand and the willingness to exploit others.

Most women are not more intelligent than you. Of course many women may be just as smart as you, and there are probably many who are indeed smarter. But for the most part, the average woman does not have an advantage over you in intelligence. Women are only able to outsmart you because of their gender advantage. They exploit the fact that you are naturally inclined to help them and give them what they want. In other words, most women can only outsmart you because you let them.

Many men are not necessarily blind to what women are doing. They simply allow it to go on. They generously give women what they want and let women feel like they are somehow smarter and more capable.

You can refuse to let women outsmart you. If you sense that a woman is trying to pull one over on you, you can refuse to play her game. Don't acknowledge her attempts to fool you or give her what she wants. Do not let her walk away feeling victorious over you. When a woman tries some sort of game or other sneaky tactic on you, call her on it. Women hate this and while they will vehemently deny your accusations, they will also know that you are onto them and they will stop trying to outsmart you.

It is important to always stay two steps ahead of women, or really anyone that you encounter. Maintain your dignity and autonomy by refusing to bend to others' will. Force people to be straight with you by dodging their attempts at manipulation. You will become a force to be reckoned with and people will treat you with more respect if you demand it.

Chapter II: How to Guard Yourself against Manipulation

There are a couple of things that you can do to guard yourself against manipulation. Beyond using the tips that I provided in Chapter I in relation to specific types of manipulation, here are some tips that you can use to steel yourself against manipulative people. These tips can be used with women or men that try to manipulate you.

Attitude

Your attitude is a huge factor in how other people see you. If you have a gentle, kind, and unassuming attitude or if you lack confidence, other people will take this as a sign of weakness and an invitation to walk all over you. You will encourage people to disrespect you and manipulate you if you project too nice of an attitude.

Instead, you need to be a little mean. I am not implying that you should treat people badly or live without a conscience. I am also not telling you to discard your kind heart. When I say "be a little mean," I actually am just telling you to command respect for yourself. This is not really mean, but most people will claim that it is. You will notice that when you start commanding respect, people will get offended and tell you that you are a mean or cold-hearted person. This is just their way of trying to manipulate you through guilt so that you start giving them what they want and letting them walk all over you again. It is OK to be mean, even if it angers manipulative people. You need to protect yourself.

Approach life and approach the people that you meet with a don't-tread-on-me attitude. Believe that you are worthy of only respect. Determine that you will not tolerate being manipulated under any circumstances. You have the right to make your own decisions about how you treat people in your life, and manipulation robs you of that right. Manipulation gets you to say yes and to do things that you are not comfortable with using a variety of emotional snares. You absolutely should not ever accept this violation of your rights. Therefore, take on the attitude that you deserve better than manipulation and stand up for yourself by refusing to accept manipulative behavior. When you spot that someone is trying to manipulate you, don't give in and don't accept their behavior. Go ahead and demand that they treat you with respect and stop manipulating you.

Be totally unapologetic, as well. You do not have to apologize to people for doing what you need to do for yourself. If you have to be selfish sometimes, then be selfish and do not apologize for it. If you have to tell someone off, then do so and don't ever say that you are sorry. Also, you do not owe anyone an explanation for why you do what you do. Just do what you feel is best for you, without worrying about what other people think. When people ask you why you act the way that you do or why you did something, just respond with, "I don't have to explain myself." Never offer an explanation for your actions, either. Your reasons for how you behave are your business and no one else's.

When you have this attitude, you will be able to stop a lot of manipulators dead in their tracks. You will cut manipulative, disrespectful, and toxic people out of your life. You will convince future manipulators that you meet that you are not an easy target and that you must be treated with respect. You will start to see that people change how they talk to you and treat you when you demand that they be respectful of your rights.

Confidence is also crucial. If you are confident, you protect yourself from people who view a lack of confidence as a sign of weakness. You also encourage people to view you in a more positive light, so that they respect you more.

Confidence is a great quality to have. Even if you do not really feel confident in yourself, pretend to be confident to others and work on believing in yourself. You really are good enough and you have every reason to be confident in who you are as a person. Eventually, you will begin to feel more confident as a direct side effect of acting like it. You will also notice significant improvements in how others treat you.

Put Yourself First

This relates to having the "mean" attitude that I just told you to adopt. You need to put yourself first, and care for yourself before all others. Of course you may wish to care for other people and do things for other people, and this is entirely your choice. But you should never sacrifice your needs for someone else.

The minute that you feel like you are going against your comfort level or somehow sacrificing your greater good for someone, stop and ask yourself why you are doing this? As a parent, husband, or community leader, you will sometimes have to sacrifice your own happiness for someone else's greater good. It is just part of the role that you have taken on. But you never *have to* do anything. You can say no. And you should say no when something does not feel right to you.

Your time and your energy carry a lot of value, no matter what others say. You have a right to conserve your time and energy for causes that really matter to you. Expending your resources on others is not necessary. In fact, it is usually a waste.

Ignore feelings of obligation. Only do things for others when you feel good about it or when you receive a positive reward for doing so that makes the effort worthwhile. Your own needs should always come first. Make sure that you take care of yourself and feel good about yourself before you do anything for others. Maybe this sounds incredibly selfish, but it is the best way to take care of yourself. Selflessness rarely behooves you in life, as you have probably learned the hard way.

Be Discerning

The most vulnerable targets for manipulators are men who do not practice discernment and who are not picky about who they associate with. These men do not take care of themselves and allow toxic people into their lives. You need to become discerning about the people that you become involved with and dedicate your time only to those who prove themselves truly worthy. This can be especially difficult when it comes to women, but being picky is actually a form of self-care that you should practice. Even when it comes to women – actually, especially when it comes to women – you should only choose to hang out with people who benefit you, care for you, and treat you with respect. Become discerning about who you let into your life and you will notice that your quality of life drastically improves.

Even if you are lonely or needy in any way, you should not just let anybody come into your life. Take your time to get to know people. Watch them for clues about how they feel about you and what their intentions are with you. Only involve yourself with people who treat you with respect and who do not actively try to manipulate you. The minute that you see someone disrespecting you or trying to manipulate you, you should either cut that person out of your life or set him or her straight with a reprimand.

Do not let women into your life just because they seem to offer something good, such as good looks or lots of sex or a stable home life. Do not even try to get romantically involved with anyone until you know the person well and see that she treats you right. You should make judgments about the women in your life based on how they treat you, nothing else. Move forward with the ones who treat you well. Never let what they seem to offer you get in the way of your discernment and make you choose to tolerate their bad behavior. Manipulators are great at promising you the world and then not delivering, so don't let their promises and offers cloud your judgment.

Offer Consequences

A great way to limit or even halt manipulation in your life is to offer solid, real consequences for manipulators. Yes, I mean that you should punish people for trying to manipulate you. You should even punish women. Manipulation is inexcusable and you should cut it short.

One consequence is to permanently cut people out of your life who just do not respect you. If someone in your life views you as a tool that he or she can use to get what he or she wants, then end the relationship. This person does not care about you, so why have him or her in your life? Don't let dependency or prior history convince you to keep toxic, disrespectful people in your life who only drain you and don't love you for who you are.

A lot of the manipulation that you will experience will come from people that do love you, however. These people do have your best interests at heart, but they get misguided along the way. Wives, children, and mothers are some of the biggest manipulators that you will ever encounter; they love you and you love them, but their behavior has gotten out of line over the years. You do not have to cut these people out of your life and you probably won't want to anyway. But you do need to set these people straight and command them to honor your rights as a human being. When you catch someone that you care about trying to manipulate you, say that you do not like being manipulated and that you must be treated with respect.

Manipulators hate being confronted. Even the kindest person in your life will object strongly to being accused of manipulation. But don't back down. Insist that you will not tolerate the particular behavior and that people need to respect your boundaries. Say that you will only do things for people who ask you directly and politely and offer you a clear choice in the matter. If this person still won't stop manipulating you, then consider not talking to him or her for a while, and continue to staunchly refuse to do what he or she is trying to get you to do.

Don't Be a Jerk Yourself

Remember the Golden Rule: Treat others as you want to be treated. You should stand up for yourself, but you should not make a habit of being a jerk to anyone and everyone for no reason. Try to be respectful and good-hearted. The better that you behave to your loved ones, the better they will behave toward you.

If you act like a real jerk all of the time, you push people away. This encourages people to dislike you and to step all over your boundaries. Being a jerk does not earn you the respect that you want; it only earns you derision and even hatred. People will manipulate you because they do not respect you and they do not believe that they can ever get their way with you. You can discourage this manipulation and encourage more honest, respectful treatment by being someone who is approachable and likable.

Again, don't confuse this with being a doormat. You need to be mean in that you need to stand up for yourself. Fiercely care for yourself and treat yourself with respect. Put yourself first. But do not act hostile or malicious to others. Treat people with the same respect that you expect from them and you will more than likely receive the same treatment back.

Chapter III: What Women Really Want

Men repeatedly wonder what women really want. It is typically a mystery that baffles most men. In no way are you here solely to please and serve women, despite how some people believe. You do not ever want to give a woman what she wants if it is at odds with your morals or your needs. Defend yourself against pushy women who expect the world from you. Serve yourself first.

However, at least half of the world population is female. That means that you constantly will have to deal with women in your life. Understanding what women really want can help you get along with women more easily. It can make your relationships with females become smoother. While you do not have to give women what they want, you can certainly cut down on a massive amount of miscommunication by developing a fundamental understanding of what women really want. You also can give women that you care about what they really want to make them happy, if you so choose.

Attention

Women really do want attention. It is not a stereotype. As a woman, I can vouch for our desire to be given attention. But I can also admit that this behavior is a bit childish. You do not have to give a woman attention all of the time. She needs to learn to occupy herself sometimes or to find attention in other people, such as her friends.

Often, women get jealous when you go out with friends because they do not feel that you have spent enough quality time with them. You may think that you have, but she doesn't see it that way. Women count conversing as spending quality time together, not doing things like watching movies or eating dinner together. I cover that more in the next section, about talking just to talk. So even if you have been with your woman all day, she may get mad when you pay other people attention because she does not feel that you have given her the proper attention. She will get mad, pout, or even compare you to other men who pay lots of attention to their wives in an attempt to manipulate you into giving her more attention.

She may even bring up sex and claim that you don't have sex with her enough, because she really just wants to feel your love and your full, undivided attention, something that she definitely gets in bed. Usually, women who bring up lack of sex just want more quality attention of any kind.

You do not have to play her games. If you feel that you have paid attention to her, then she will just have to deal with you spending time with other guys. However, it is not a bad thing to pay attention to the women in your life. Everyone that you care about deserves some of your time and effort. Keep your relationships healthy by showing her some true quality time.

Put away your phone, shut off the TV, and talk just to talk.

Talking Just to Talk

Women communicate for different reasons than men. Conversation is a form of bonding for women. When a woman sits down with you and starts talking about her awful day, she is just talking to vent and to bond with you. She is not looking for you to solve her problems. So stop offering advice or getting frustrated when you cannot seem to help her work out what she is going through. She is just looking to you to listen to her, not to fix things for her.

Women want to just spend some time talking with you every day. You can really help a woman feel better about her relationship with you if you oblige her desire to talk just to talk. You might not see the point of it, but keep in mind that she does. You will cut down on a lot of jealousy, whining, nagging, and manipulation for attention if you simply dedicate a little bit of time to simply conversing with the woman in your life.

Security

Women love to feel secure. They often rely on men for at least part of their security. While you are not responsible for your woman's happiness, you should at least try to help her feel secure in her relationship with you. It is part of your duty as her partner in life. She will start freaking out, acting "crazy," and being bitchy toward you if she does not feel secure. She may even start trying to manipulate you into giving her the security she craves because she does not know how to communicate what she really needs to you. This manipulation will manifest as nagging, flattery, jealousy, crying, and other actions that drive you nuts.

You can eliminate these feelings and her crazy behavior by offering her some security. All you have to do is show her that you love her and that you don't plan on ditching her. Show her some affection. Go ahead and make her feel like your queen by telling her that she is the most beautiful woman in your life and that you love only her. Also, do something thoughtful, such as surprising her with flowers, to show that you do think about her throughout the day. A little bit of affection goes a long way in placating a woman's insecurities. Showing her a little bit of love will calm her down and make her very happy. Your relationship will become more stable and peaceful if you take just a little time out of each day to offer her some reassurance of your life. This is just basic relationship maintenance that every man should perform if he wants a happy, healthy home life.

Alternatively, you can just move on to someone who is more secure in herself and does not rely on you for security. While this is your prerogative, just remember that any and all women that you get romantically involved with will start depending on you for at least some reassurance about the relationship. It is the nature of relationships for women to start giving part of themselves to you, and thus to start relying on you for some love and security. Be prepared to give this security as a romantic partner or else deal with annoying arguments, manipulative behavior, and bad break-ups with unsatisfied women for the rest of your life.

I do want to add that you are not responsible for any woman's ego. There is a huge difference between giving a woman security in your relationship by reassuring her that you love her, and constantly assuaging a woman who does not believe in herself. If you wind up with a woman who needs you to make her feel good about herself, then I suggest moving on and finding someone more secure. Her identity should be strong independent of you; she should be secure enough to believe in herself and not burden you with the chore of constantly feeding her fragile ego. She should not need you just to feel whole or good about herself. While it does not hurt to tell your woman that she looks good and is doing well as a girlfriend or wife to you, you should not have to tell her these things constantly just to make her believe that she is worth something. You also should not have to deal with arguments and jealousy that a woman starts just because she is too insecure to handle the existence of other attractive women in the world.

Just don't deal with this. Move on from overly clingy, insecure women, as they will not change and they will just drag you down to their miserable level over time. They will also constantly disrespect you by manipulating you to give them the confidence and the security that they should be giving themselves.

Feeling Needed and Wanted

Women want to feel needed and wanted. This appeals to their nurturing instincts. Nothing makes a woman feel more heated than when she senses that she does not matter. Sadly, even in our modern progressive society, a lot of women find themselves pushed to the wayside. This makes women get very petty or irate.

If you want a happy woman in your life, show her that you love her, need her, and want her. Take some time out of the day to ask her how she is doing and to give her a kiss. These small actions will make a world of difference.

Ask Women Direct Questions

You know that you cannot read minds. When you try, you usually get it wrong, right?

You can avoid all of this trouble by actually asking women direct questions. If you are unclear about what a woman is telling you or asking you, then ask her. Most women will actually appreciate this and they will tell you clearly so that you can avoid misunderstandings.

The same advice goes for assumptions. Never assume what a woman means or what she is thinking. Never assume that she means a certain thing by any of her actions. If you have doubts, ask her. Be an adult and communicate clearly with her. You can lead the way toward healthy adult communication by facilitating good communication and taking steps to avoid miscommunication. You can also set a healthy model for the relationship's communication yourself.

Be the bigger person and start asking direct questions instead of assuming and mind reading.

Chapter IV: How to Heal from a Manipulative Woman

Some manipulation is normal in almost every human relationship. You will inevitably encounter manipulation more than once in your life. But some women are so manipulative and awful that you have now been deeply hurt, and you do not feel like you can trust anyone anymore. It can certainly be hard to trust again after being around someone who constantly had hidden motives and who shamelessly used you to attain her unknown ends. However, not all women are this way. It is important for you to heal from your trust issues and move on to a woman who cares about you and does not manipulate you so shamelessly.

Society likes to claim that big boys don't cry and that men should not have feelings. We both know that this just isn't true. It is possible for you to be hurt. To add insult to injury, you probably also feel embarrassed that you are so hurt and that you let a manipulator get the best of you. It is OK to feel all of these things. But it not OK to suffer in silence forever. You deserve to heal and feel a lust for life again. Therefore, read on to learn how to heal from the wounds that some really horrible people can inflict upon you.

Acknowledge Your Feelings

As a man, you are probably adept at compartmentalizing things. When something bad happens in your personal life, you file it away and focus on other things, like work. But you cannot truly resolve emotional wounds and get over trust issues to lead a healthy, happy life if you repress or ignore your emotions. Take a little bit of time out of your day to really just feel how hurt you are. It is never pleasant to face your true emotions about traumas or heartbreak, but doing so lets you facilitate the healing process. Acknowledge that you feel the way that you do, and don't feel bad for how you feel. You have a right to feel so hurt. What this person did to you is not OK. You should never feel this badly because of another human being. If you do, then that person is in the wrong.

Stop Blaming Yourself

Victims tend to find fault in their own actions. But a victim is rarely, if ever, at fault. What this woman did to you is not your fault. It is all her fault. There is something wrong with her, not with you.

Don't think that you did anything to make her act this way toward you. Any woman who uses men without remorse has a serious issue, possibly even sociopathy, and she will prey on any victim. You did not do anything to trigger or deserve her behavior. You are not inadequate and you did not kill her love or make her fall out of love with you. You may recall some messed up things that you did to her as well, but understand that she could have just confronted you or left you if you were so bad to her. She did not need to rip your heart out. She tolerated your bad treatment of her just to use you for some end of her own. Your poor treatment of her is not the reason that she did this to you, and it does not justify or negate the severity of her wrongdoing either.

Don't feel stupid for falling for this woman. You may beat yourself up, wondering why you fell for her tricks, and why you even hooked up with her in the first place. Stop doing this. Manipulators can be really charming. She was able to fool you, but it is not because you are stupid. In fact, you are probably a very kind person, which is a great quality even though it makes you vulnerable to bad people.

Confront the Person

A confrontation can help you get things off of your chest. You can write down what you want to say and either call her or see her in person, if you are still on speaking terms. Tell her how you really feel.

Manipulators and sociopaths never feel remorse. You probably will not get an apology. In fact, the manipulator may just start to manipulate you some more to make you feel like you are the one at fault. Don't fall for this. You are not at fault. Just walk away before the manipulator can argue with you.

Have Zero Contact

Better yet, skip the confrontation altogether and just have radio silence. Cut this person out of your life completely. You do not need such harmful people in your life, so don't even waste any more time with this woman. You are better off without her. You can also heal more quickly if she is not in your life anymore.

Confrontation is acceptable if you really feel the need to say something to her. But if you do confront her, make sure that it is your very last interaction with her. Do not see her or speak to her again after you state your final piece.

Cold turkey lack of contact can be really difficult to adjust to. You will miss her. You will want to confront her. You will think about her a lot. With time, these feelings will fade and you will move on.

Use This as a Learning Experience

There are positives to every negative in life. Maybe some evil woman ripped your heart out and put it in a blender for fun, but you have survived. Now you can learn from this experience. At least let this experience serve some purpose in your life by using it to better yourself and protect yourself in the future.

Use this experience to get to know yourself. Figure out what is not cool with you. Using this knowledge, you can start setting boundaries that will protect you in the future from other manipulative and emotionally abusive women.

Also, use this experience to learn what to watch out for. Avoid women like the one who hurt you. If you start to develop an eerie sense of déjà vu when dating someone new, consider that this person may be reminding you of your ex and then run far, far away. Remember the different things your ex did to you and watch for the same behavior in other people that you meet.

You probably have a lot of built-up anger toward your ex. You may have speeches in your mind of things that you wish you could have said to her as she used you. Well, use these speeches as frameworks for how you will confront and tell off other manipulators in your life. Let your anger against her out by defending your own honor and human rights.

Remember Not All Women are the Same

It can be easy to never want to trust someone again. But remember that not all women are the same. Now that you have been through hell with one woman, you can use that experience to become discerning and weed out manipulative, hurtful women in the future. You can thus find yourself a really good, kind woman who does not try to use you and hurt you. It is important to let go of trust issues and acknowledge the fact that not everyone is as bad as your ex was.

Conclusion

Women often run circles around men. Centuries of gender subjugation has made women feel like manipulation is the only real way to gain control over men and have their needs met. Also, some women inadvertently perform manipulation as a way to satisfy their needs, since they cannot effectively communicate with men what they really need. Finally, some women out there are just pathological and manipulate you just for their own toxic thrills.

But you have rights as a human being. You do not deserve or need manipulation. Manipulation is a flagrant violation of your basic human rights. Do not tolerate it anymore. Even if a woman is manipulating you for innocent reasons, you do not have to accept this. Teach her healthier ways to talk to you and interact with you.

It is important to stick up for yourself. Set up some boundaries against manipulation. Erect a metaphorical fence around you that deters manipulators. The minute that you spot manipulative behavior in someone, put an end to the behavior. Become pickier about who you associate with and always tend to your needs before you tend to someone else's. Don't feel bad or apologize for saying no, because saying no is your human right.

There are many key behaviors that indicate that a woman is trying to manipulate you. The minute that you spot any of these behaviors, go ahead and put an end to it. Don't fall for women's games. You should defend yourself and deflect any and all manipulation. By doing this, you protect yourself and you teach others how to better act around you.

Sometimes, you need to give a little to get a little. If you are in any kind of relationship, you may find that giving your woman some forms of security and affection will really make her happier. As a direct result, she will treat you better and make you happier. But you are not obligated to do anything for anyone. You can refuse to tend to anyone's needs or satisfy anyone's demands. It is up to you.

When you encounter manipulation, you should put an end to it. Purge your life free of toxic, manipulative women. Sadly, sometimes you will find that a manipulative woman really hurts you. Your feelings matter too, no matter what society says. Maybe big boys don't cry, but you can feel hurt. So it is important to take steps to heal yourself from the harmful effects of really manipulative and horrible women. Start tending to yourself and facilitating healing now. Don't bury or repress your hurt and tell yourself to just get over it because this is not helpful at all in healing your wounds for the long-term.

The best part of healing is emerging from the experience as a stronger person. A woman may have gotten the best of you and scarred you before, but now you are better able to pick good women and avoid harm. You also know more about how to please women, since this book has given you a fundamental understanding of what women really want. Stop spending time with manipulators and instead start spending time with real women who are not out to hurt you or use you. Take care of yourself by putting yourself first and setting healthy boundaries on the women in your life.

Take control of your life now. Stop letting women run circles around you. You deserve better treatment than that. Even in today's feminist age, you still deserve respect. Don't let anyone take your right to be treated with respect away from you. Women do not have to subjugate themselves to you in this day and age, but they do have to respect you. Start enjoying that respect by commanding it for yourself now.

Thank you for reading.

Other books available by Blaine Williams on Kindle, paperback and audio:

Self-Healing 101: How to Emotionally Heal Yourself and Methodically Solve your Problems without the Use of Traditional Therapy